IONA

The Other Island

Words by Kenneth Steven
Photographs by Iain Sarjeant

SAINT ANDREW PRESS
Edinburgh

First published in 2014 by
SAINT ANDREW PRESS
121 George Street
Edinburgh EH2 4YN

ISBN 978-0-86153-830-0

British Library Cataloguing in Publication Data
A catalogue record for this book is available from the British Library.

It is the publisher's policy to only use papers that are natural and recyclable and that have been manufactured from timber grown in renewable, properly managed forests. All of the manufacturing processes of the papers are expected to conform to the environmental regulations of the country of origin.

Typeset by Iain Sarjeant.

Printed and bound in the United Kingdom by Ashford Colour Press, Gosport, Hants.

Contents

Iona THE OTHER ISLAND

This book grew out of a shared vision. Both Iain Sarjeant and I had known Iona from childhood; we had been fortunate enough to be brought to the island summer after summer. All the Hebridean landfalls are special in their unique ways; it's hard to describe those particular individual characteristics without using a great number of words. As shorthand, I like to think of it as varying colours; each colour has a different shade.

But Iona, for many at least, has something more, something deeper. It is an island that has a profound impact on people, whether they are inherently spiritually minded or not. George MacLeod, the founder of the Iona Community, and the man responsible for the re-building of the Abbey last century, described Iona as a thin place. Somehow the veil was thin between this world and God's. There are many who believe the centuries of prayer whispered in the Abbey stones is what brings that very thinness, and yet that is somehow rendering this quality man-made, and limiting it to one corner of the island. There was more than likely a reason for Columba's choosing of Iona, not only because it lay right at the heart of the emerging Celtic kingdom, a stepping stone between Ireland and the country that was to become Scotland. We are told it was an island of druids and, therefore, once upon a time it had been chosen by them too for a reason. So the power of Iona – and even the origins of its name – is shrouded in mystery. This story has to be about the whole island rather than one particular, special corner.

I go back in my mind to when I was three or four years old. I vividly remember arriving at Fionnphort with my parents and having my first glimpse of Iona. There was the ferry nodding by the jetty. Even now, forty years later, I am moved to write those words. I visited all manner of other Hebridean islands with my parents, but none could compare with the overwhelming power of this place and all that it meant.

And all that it meant. Those are crucial words, because I somehow felt the same wonderment that I experienced in the Abbey cloister as I did at Columba's Bay or at Port Ban. There was no schism between the formally religious places and all the myriad other places I knew and loved elsewhere on Iona.

Near the North End

That was the starting point of this book for Iain and me, the shared desire to tell the story of those many other corners through images and words. Both of us knew all too well that so many thousand pilgrims visit each year, particularly in July and August, and simply have time to walk from the village to the Abbey and back again. The next place on their itinerary is already beckoning; the buses over at Fionnphort are waiting to whisk them back across Mull.

Iain and I were also aware that so many of the books on Iona are about the story of the island's top right-hand corner alone. Not that we would want for a moment to take away from the wonder and power of Abbey and Nunnery, it's just that sometimes a reader who had never visited the island would have the impression this really is all that's to be found here!

There's perhaps a further reason for the creation of this book. One of the rather lovely evolutions of a writing genre or sub-genre over recent years has been in respect of micro-worlds. The looking at one type of flower, one particular season

or mountain or even field. Often this writing has an environmental core to it; often too there is a meticulous detailing of the subject. It is as though it is put under a kind of loving microscope. This writing is perhaps a backlash against the kind of contemporary guides that seek to sum up a city or even a whole country with a few throwaway lines. It is saying that small really is beautiful and exciting, that spending time slowing down and leaving the mad rush of this world's frenetic pace reaps rich rewards.

This book is for those who come to Iona for that brief summer hour and are in danger of leaving feeling let down and disillusioned by the experience. It is for those who have known Iona well and have fallen in love with its many secret corners, and who want to remember and re-visit them. And it is for those who may not have been aware of the existence of those corners, and who want to return to make their own journeys to find them.

A word on exploration of Iona's wilder corners. There are places where very real care needs to be taken; don't be beguiled by the benign Iona that meets you when you land on a warm June morning. The south-east and south-west corners in particular have headlands and coves that offer real challenge to the best of walkers. It's also very easy to get lost in both the north and south of the island where the terrain is all quite similar – confusingly so. When on the island for the writing of this book, I set out one day for the Port of the Young Lad's Rock. I must have struck off far too early and ended up wandering about on crags to the north of it. In the end I decided that discretion was the better part of valour and simply came back to do better planning. That hurt my pride, because I know Iona well. But don't make the mistake of thinking it's a tiny island that's easily covered in a couple of days: that's the whole intention of the creation of this book. It's much bigger than you think. And if you're better off enjoying the truly rugged corners from the safety of an armchair with this book, then good and well.

N

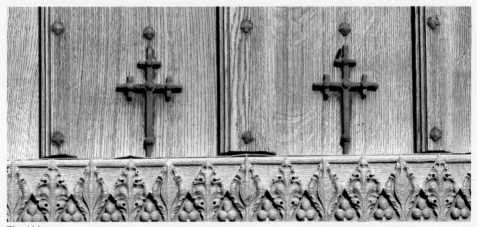

The Abbey

The Abbey cloisters

For the Book of Kells

We know that inks used for the illuminated pages of the Book of Kells were brought from far away. We know, too, that it's likely the Book – surely one of the great treasures of the Celtic Christian world – was begun on Iona and then taken to Ireland for safe-keeping during the years of the Viking raids.

Five months after leaving a far language and a strange land
under the soft nightfall of August and a fine rain –
the sea smooth and a fur moon full in the northern sky.

Five months after the ravages of pirates
(one vial broken by storm,
another bartered for fresh well water):
when thirst had thickened tongues to madness.

Five months after seas that held their breath,
that would not move, were made of silence,
that oar by oar were fought to cross.

This simple cove of rocks
and monks who grateful come to share the lifting;
to bring this cargo safe at last
for love of letters.

Traigh Mor – THE BIG BEACH

It deserves a better name, in Gaelic and in English, especially when the island has such a wealth of evocative names for hills and glens and other beaches. But what it lacks in name, it more than makes up for in attractiveness. And even if walking is a struggle, reaching Traigh Mor should be possible for most. It is so near and yet so far. I associate the beach with toddlers learning to walk (since that's who one sees here most often in the summer, and since it's here I learned to walk myself).

At low tide, a whole host of little boomerangs of smaller beach appear, all laced with minute worlds of shells. There are other beaches on the island that have such 'lacings', but none has cowrie shells as Traigh Mor does. They are little pink things the size of a child's fingernail. When sitting up on the sand, so to speak, they're just skin-coloured hummocks. Little bottoms. But underneath they have a 'zip' that stretches from one end to the other; an opening that reveals the inner, empty chamber of the shell. They are only one type of shell among many to be found on Traigh Mor; over a half hour of hunting one might hope to collect twenty or thirty. They're easiest to find at low tide when all these beautiful stretches of shells have been left exposed.

The Eastern Edge

Even if you can't walk far, walk here. Leave the village by turning left at the jetty, right down past the war memorial and the first beach that in my childhood was known as Coal Bay. I can remember the coal being unloaded here, and it's a fine little horseshoe of beach in and of itself. A place of happiness in high summer, with children tottering about at the water's edge, and chasing dogs, and on days of cold brightness, of folk hunkered down in the sand dunes to escape the wind and find the sun.

But down beyond here, further on this east side road, there are all manner of little tiny coves that appear at low tide. Beaches that have no names but which are filled with luminous blue water washing whitest sand. Little wonder that the Scottish Colourists, the great painters of the early twentieth century, came out to Iona to capture these wild and beautiful hues.

These are places to sit a while in quiet. It may be that patient waiting will be rewarded by an otter, for they are here on the east side of Iona and I've seen them. But otters are not to be ordered. I spent the first years of my life trailing Hebridean beaches desperately hoping I would see one. In the end I gave up in despair. And then I saw one.

Martyr's Bay (or 'Coal Bay')

The Glen of the Temple

Sometimes even now there are places I can't find:
Caves that go missing, beaches I search for that are lost –
There are times the island is bigger inside.
Once, as a child, I came down into the Glen of the Temple
All on my own. Everything was still around me.
The air hummed and fluttered with living things
And I realised I couldn't see the sea, and for a moment
All the points of the compass jumbled
And I was in the middle, the very middle of the island,
In the middle of summer. And I wasn't afraid.

out of that battered coast
and all the winter can throw

the days of flurrying snow
and the wind searching

the long and starless nights
high seas and the power gone

the spring comes suddenly
in the twirling song of a lark

a torn blue sky and the light
here and there in fragments

the jewellery of flowers
reds and blues and golds

rising from among the rocks
year after faithful year.

Can anyone dare to say
they do not believe in miracles?

Sandeels Bay

When the tide's at its very lowest, it's quite possible to reach Sandeels by walking round the headlands and the beaches from Traigh Mor. But that's not for the faint-hearted, nor is it a journey that's to be taken too lightly. Being stranded by an incoming tide could be nasty indeed.

And the inland path, for the most part, is easy and fine to follow. Walk down the track that lies just up from Traigh Mor. That leads to a gate and once through (it's very much for public access) walk across the field at the top of the next beach. You will most likely be among sheep peacefully grazing.

A stream flows down onto the beach, at the far side where the ground starts rising up quite sharply. The burn should be easy to cross in any one of several places, and beyond, a rough track curves round and up through the hummocks. That track then turns to lead over a grassy plateau, south once more. After some minutes of walking you'll see the thickly ivied ramparts of a rock ledge on the right-hand side. They rise perhaps fifty or more feet, and on the other side are sand dunes and marram grass. The path will lead down past old farm machinery and through to the top of Sandeels Bay.

The name is very appropriate. If you creep along the tide's edge (or in high summer take off your shoes and socks to brave the bright water), you're more than likely to see shoals of eels nipping the tide's edge. Most likely it's but a fraction of those that once were here, but I have rejoiced over the numbers that I've seen in recent years nonetheless.

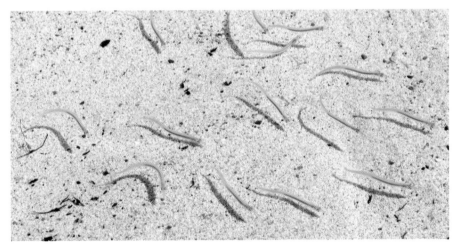

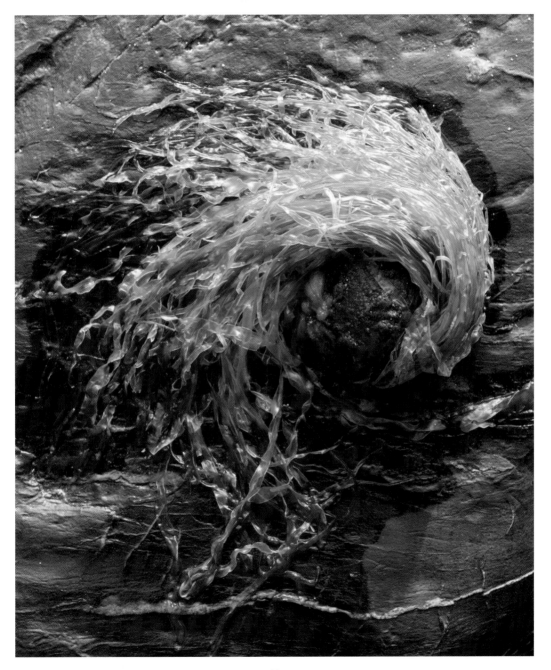

Sandeels Bay may not seem terribly exciting for the hunter of stones or shells, but don't write it off too quickly. Little necklaces of small stones are always there, close to the tide's edge. And often enough tiny pieces of marble and serpentine are to be found, and cowrie shells. There are fragments of sea glass too (sometimes uncannily akin to the translucent pieces of serpentine known as Columba's Tears). There is something about the glass that gives them away: one tell-tale edge that's not natural enough, too great a clarity when you hold them up to the light. The pieces of serpentine almost always have little flecks of quartz in them.

This is a place for a fire and songs on a summer evening. It's a sheltered beach, facing east and therefore protected on a day when the prevailing wind is strong. But beware those ramparts and their ivy walls; you may be tempted to find a way up and through to continue exploring south, but it's wild walking indeed. Better to go back inland and follow the paths, not the wandering of endless sheep tracks through many a treacherous bog.

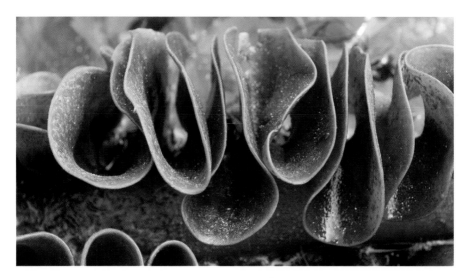

The Story

That Good Friday, after we had scattered
From the booming echoes of the Abbey
Out into wild night
Everything etched against silver
And the islands round about
Asleep in restless sea

I thought what it must have been like
In an occupied country
The story ended in defeat –
Nails and spears and wailing –
How they must have gone home hopeless
Thinking the whole thing over,
And how it had just begun.

The West

Even if getting to some of the edge places described in this book proves impossible, reaching the west will not be. The road from the village leads down the east side of the island, hugging the shore, until suddenly and sharply it turns a corner and heads straight west to the Machair. So of course it can be reached with a car. And there's an alternative. The road that leads up through the village, past the nunnery, the telephone box and school, then turns left through a gate and winds up over the hill past a couple of farms to come down to join the same road west.

Here in front of you, however you may arrive, is the wonderfully named Bay at the Back of the Ocean. A great curving of rocky shores, busy with birdlife, above which is machair, one of those wonderful Gaelic descriptions for which at least ten English words are needed. Machair is the rich meadow above the tideline which is effectively growing out of shell sand. If you look all around your feet as you walk down from the gate here at the west you will see hundreds of tiny white snail shells in the sand-flecked grass.

This was a place that my father loved. For any birdwatcher it is a paradise. And this sweeping scimitar of beach is a real size, and that was something that mattered to my father. On Iona everything was generally on too small a scale for him, but here was a place that opened its shoulders, that was wide and needed time to explore.

Most of all perhaps, the Machair and the Bay at the Back of the Ocean are to be visited on evenings when the sun goes down in greatest splendour. It is a natural amphitheatre of epic proportions. Great tassels of vivid red and orange setting the sky on fire above the headlands of Tiree. All the special effects of Hollywood can't start to rival this.

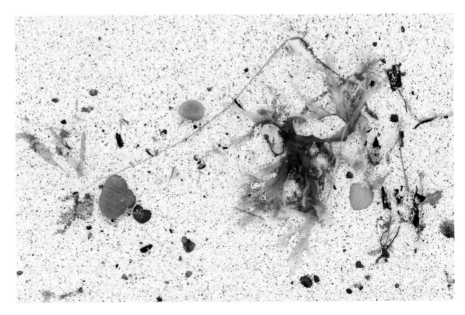

*'here was a
place that
opened its
shoulders, that
was wide and
needed time to
explore'*

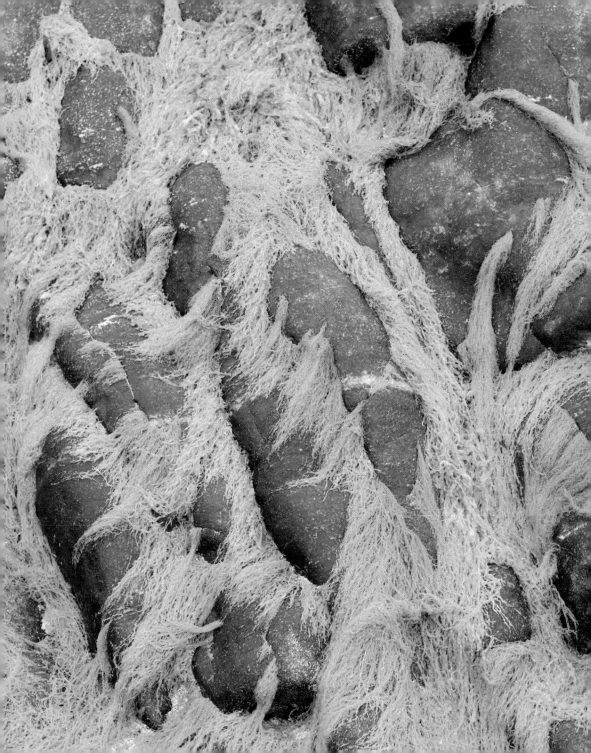

Port Ban

You can never quite get used to arriving at Port Ban. Even going through the green heart of Iona can't prepare you for the sheer light: the white gold of the sand and the translucence of the water beyond. That water is almost clear, without any blue or green at all, because of the shell sand beneath. Two great sheltering arms of rocky headland to north and south make of Port Ban what must be the finest lagoon in all the Hebrides: perhaps it is the sheer darkness of the surrounding rocks that renders the beach and water so startlingly and hauntingly beautiful. In the summer that water warms; the pale shallow pool is strummed with sunlight and becomes utterly safe to swim. Up at the top of the beach in the shell sand there's a myriad of tiny shells: mussels and scallops and fronds of coral and fragments of sea urchin all the size of a baby's fingernail.

Columba's Bay

The highlight of every holiday on Iona was the day at St Columba's Bay. Rucksacks and bags were prepared; finally we set off. There was the crossing of the island to the Machair, then after turning left beyond the gate we kept to the fence, all the way down past the edge of one solitary house to the beginning of the climb into the wilds. My parents liked to call the toughest part of the walk, up the rocky track to the loch, the Khyber Pass. It's not for the faint-hearted on miserable days; it's a slow slog that's at its worst if there's been long rain. Then there are one or two wide pools to navigate, until finally you reach the top and can look back and take in the view to the west.

Of course there can be days when the west is nothing more than rain! But when it's clear, there are the strange shapes of the Treshnish Isles: the Dutchman's Cap, Lunga and a scattering of other jagged islets that are all the result of Mull's great volcanic eruption. Then beyond, on a good day, is the long, low line of the island of Coll. And when the visibility is at its best, to the north of Mull you'll see the islands of Rum and Eigg and even Skye itself.

Once the steep climb is completed, all that remains is the descent to the Bay. The path is much improved; I can well remember the fight through bits of bog until the struggle down to the lovely lush glen above the Bay was completed. Now it's an easy walk until the path leads you to a notch of rocks and one last steep drop to the bracken and deep grass of the glen. Thereafter keep left, and carry straight on until you can go no further. Here is Columba's Bay.

Once upon a time I kept my own tradition of running down that glen until I'd reached the rocks. I still feel the strange holding power of that place all these years later, though gone are the days for running its length. It's like a green bowl, womb-like and safe, and with a mystery that cannot be defined. Sometimes as adults we sense the loss of something that was mysterious in childhood; here, for me, is a place that has never changed.

I inherited the joy of searching for green stones from my mother. It's not the only beach on Iona where polished pebbles and fragments of serpentine are to be found – it's not even necessarily the best (though it's where my best stones are from). But it's the most famous, not least because of the tradition that it was here Columba and his monks landed. There are two kinds of hunters for green stones: sifters and tide-dancers. My mother was of the former group and I of the latter. Sifting meant just that; sitting at a certain point of the beach beside deep piles of smaller stones and meticulously turning them in the hope of catching a flash of green.

I hadn't the patience for that and I still don't. I would go along the tide edge, for all the world like a heron, waiting to stab. It involved a considerable amount of risk if the tide was coming in; that sudden seventh wave might take you by surprise and drench you. But if I'd found my treasure, I didn't mind.

How do you tell marble from serpentine? It takes a little time to learn the difference, but it's fairly simple. Pebbles of marble are generally made up of bands of green and black and dark red; when under water they look smooth and shiny. But as soon as they're brought up from the water they turn dull; they can't be polished in the hand.

There's a far wider range of pebbles that are made of pure serpentine or have serpentine in them. On the beaches of the south-east corner of Iona you'll find chunks of white stone with bright green flecks: that's one type. There there are pebbles that contain serpentine; the colour can range from dark green through to a bluish-green or even a blood red. If you're really lucky you'll find the kind of serpentine pebbles I've treasured from childhood days: pure dark green stones, the green that of a summer leaf or a caterpillar. But what really distinguishes a pebble of serpentine from a piece of marble is the ability to polish it; the oils of the hand will transform a serpentine pebble in seconds so it looks and feels as though it has been tumbled. It will gain a sheen that a similar looking bit of marble will never acquire.

Of course you may be like my father and not have the patience to be either a sifter or a tide-dancer. Whenever I go to St Columba's Bay now I can imagine him up on a headland, on one side of the bay or the other, his binoculars relentlessly searching the waves for birds. He was too restless to look for stones.

But he would come back to join the picnic. Even in high summer there's wood to be found on the beach; we'd make a fire on the west side in the shelter of the rocks, fill the old kettle with fresh water and brew jet black tea. The day's adventure was composed of many parts; all of those parts made up the magic of the whole.

I like the Iona Community tradition of throwing one stone back to the waves before leaving St Columba's Bay. It's a way of shedding something we want to leave behind; it involves stopping and thinking about just where we are in our journey and considering what's weighing us down and holding us back.

Sometimes I feel I know even now when it's time to go. I'll find a certain piece of serpentine and feel sure that were I to search for hours I'd not find anything as good, far less better. But no matter how special that piece of green stone may be, I know I'll be back just the same. And it's not just about the finding; it's about the journey.

There are a whole cluster of little coves in the south-east corner of the island, all worthy of discovery and exploration. I find it easiest to reach those closest to St Columba's Bay by a little path that cuts through from the glen above it. Walk up from the Bay, a labyrinth etched in the grass in boulders to your right. About a hundred yards further on, there's a cut in the ramparts of the hilly ground on that right-hand side. Watch your footing, especially during the monsoon season, because the lower section can be boggy indeed. Once you've reached higher ground, keep on through, following that grassy cleft which runs pretty much straight as an arrow. The first beach, steeply down below on your right-hand side, is the Port of Ivor's Cornfield. I remember 'discovering' it in younger days and struggling down its steep sides in the certain belief that the shore below would be positively deep and green with serpentine treasures. I was disappointed. Although it's effectively round the corner from that easternmost edge of Columba's Bay (always the place where I've found the best treasures) it was surprisingly devoid of good stones. There were plenty of other things, and the tiny polished beads of serpentine called Columba's Tears, but not the treasure trove I had envisaged. I struggled back up to the top half an hour later thinking little of the Port of Ivor's Cornfield, but a few years on I decided to try again and was rewarded with a great knuckle of green stone that was more than worth discovering.

A little cave of green stone
Smoothed by centuries of sea
To a pebble small as a pinkie nail
Chanced up out of the waves' reach.

Hold it to light and it changes
Becomes a globe of fractures
A cavern of ledges and glinting
Not one green but many at once.

And suddenly I think of it bigger
As the whole of the human heart
Carrying the cuts of its journey
Brokenness letting in light.

The Gully of Pat's Cow

The Gully of Pat's Cow is one of the most alluring locations on the island, and one of the most dauntingly inaccessible. Perhaps it was partly the name that spun a web of magic about me to begin with. It would be lovely to know the story of the derivation.

Instead of going down to the Port of Ivor's Cornfield, continue walking through on the path that leads from the glen and St Columba's Bay. Walk right through to the other side. You'll recognise the Gully of Pat's Cow because it has a very real beach at the bottom of it; don't ever be tempted by neighbouring gullies that are quite impenetrable. The only real way down into the Gully of Pat's Cow is at the point you first reach. A series of natural steps leads to a table-top of rock, and from there it's an easy few further steps to the sand. Work out the descent carefully; it's not worth risking an ankle or leg.

At low tide there's a lovely tiny beach out at the end of the gully. On both sides you're enclosed by rock walls rising ten and more feet. The shingly beach always has its share of green treasures (mainly because so few people know about the place or bother to visit).

I'm pretty certain that it's also a place for tiny polished globes of Baltic amber. I was given a piece as a child (which I still have and treasure), and I know for sure it came from Iona, and certainly too from one of the coves in the south-east corner. It's a beautiful thing, like a frozen piece of honey, and translucent. It turns into pure gold in the sunlight.

The Gully of Pat's Cow is somewhere to visit to escape from the weight of the world. It has a very special magic, but find it on the first occasion at least in the company of someone else.

The Marble Quarry

I know many people (including my sister, who led a climbing expedition to Greenland) who have managed to lose the marble quarry. The hinterland of the south-east corner is confusingly similar; directions can easily be muddled. The criss-crossing of sheep tracks with human ones leads to obvious puzzling, and on days when the mists are low there can be further confusion.

The marble quarry is somewhere I've seldom tried to find; partly for the reasons stated above, and partly also because it's not a place that terribly attracts me. I'm immediately aware of the many for whom it's quite the opposite, a place of very real significance – somewhere that's part of the Iona pilgrimage. The broken cottages of the men who worked the quarry are somewhat ghostly to me; the old rusting machinery eerie and ugly.

But this is a place that is fundamentally part of the Iona story too, and ignoring it would be wrong. It must have been a hard life indeed for the men who chiselled out great rocks of marble for transport by boat to be carved into many famous and fabulous creations. It's worth pausing at the ghosts of these houses and thinking about those lives.

At night their voices and their laughter warmed these walls. The moth white of lamps. There was music too, the nights the fiddle played and voices sang. They would have laboured hard and they'd have played hard too. They wrote their story here, in these walls.

there are Januarys when being modern means nothing:
the telegraph wires are whipped like skipping ropes
the sea is an impossible crossing

everything is back to the beginning;
about an open fire and books,
waiting patiently for days of storm to pass

then this place is an island once again –
every bit as much and more than in the days
they carried back the news from coracles

The Port of the Young Lad's Rock

The Port of the Young Lad's Rock is another of the elusive places on Iona's edge. I have lost it more often than I have found it, but there is a relatively reliable route (I qualify my assertion only because outwith the summer season, when the ground is often very boggy, this route may be difficult to follow).

My starting point was the loch. I kept to the left (the east) side when walking; just beyond it a fence runs off due east, probably marking a very ancient boundary wall. I followed the fence until I could clearly see the Sound of Iona and the Ross of Mull beyond; eventually the old boundary wall becomes visible and curves round to the south-east. This almost points the way down to the Port of the Young Lad's Rock. Even in high summer, after weeks of sun, I found this little glen boggy. As much as possible, keep to higher ground.

Because it's seldom visited, there are often good green stones to be found. Once down on the beach (composed of boulders and shingle) one feels held in a sanctuary. There's no other way in (except by little less than rock climbing; the ramparts on either side are sheer and not to be treated lightly), other than by the gullet of water itself – once I met a party of canoeists who had paddled over that morning from Mull. And the safest way back is to retrace one's steps and follow wall and fence back up to the loch. Short-cuts seldom if ever are on Iona.

The South West Corner

For exploring the secret corners and coves of the south west, I find it easiest to go up onto the Cairn of the Back to Ireland. I begin by walking to the loch (the only one on the island) and then turning off to the right along the north side of it. The path curls round and up onto hillier ground, and then I head south-west, across the Hill of the Lambs and down into the hollow below. It's a long slog up to the ramparts of the Cairn of the Back to Ireland, but it's well worth having the height to work out directions.

From there on a clear day the whole south coast of Iona would seem easily walked. It doesn't look far to St Columba's Bay, and as the crow flies it isn't. But crows don't have to navigate bogs and rocky outcrops; they're not disorientated by mist and demoralised by drizzle. Once you lose the high ground, directions can quickly be lost or confused.

The Port of the Marten-Cat Cliff

The Port of the Marten-Cat Cliff intrigued me as much for its name as anything else. Iain and I decided to visit it on one of the days we were on the island at the same time. From here, views to any number of other islands are clear on the right days: Islay, Jura and Colonsay almost straight ahead; Tiree, Coll and the Treshnish Isles to the west; Eigg, Rum and Skye to the north at the very best of times.

The Port of the Marten-Cat Cliff was pretty much below us. There's no easy way down; it's a steep descent into the stony bay. I don't think bogginess was a problem so much as hidden hollows that might leave an ankle badly twisted or even broken. We came down slowly, contouring the rocky slopes and right away remarking on the sheer profusion of botanic species on every side.

In fact, apart from the fairly unsurprising amount of green-flecked stones on the beach, that was the biggest joy of the place. Among Iain's list of finds were roseroot, juniper, wood sage, St John's Wort, ragged robin, eyebright, self-heal and bog asphodel. Mentioning them all in the context of this hidden bay gives the impression this is the one and only location for them; that's certainly not the case. Nor would this be naming all that's to be found on the island.

Iain stayed for a spectacular sunset and was thrilled by the aerial displays of peregrine falcons. It was apparent parent birds were teaching their very vocal youngster to fly. Once down at the shoreline here you're aware of the very real and wonderful wildness of Iona's south-west corner. In the middle of the island you simply wouldn't imagine that Iona possessed such truly dramatic edges.

This for a toothache and that to ease
The long night of a girl in birthing
To reap things for a child's foot
Or bathe the sickness from an old wound.

The little snippets out of this hollow
Plucked from beside a clattering stream
Brought home and boiled, gathered in drops,
For safe keeping, for the winter's dark.

Juniper

Looking Forward

When I am going to Iona by bus
I like to creep in to a window seat
And watch Mull flickering past.
I am looking forward: I want the journey over
Yet I hold what lies ahead like warm light.
Mull is made of great darkenings,
Sudden flickerings of late October sun;
Red deer battling, the colour of bracken,
Over hillsides that are made of rock.
The burns like tousled collies;
The ben with a shivering of snow.
Then, at last, after an hour and a half,
The island there in the top right corner of the window
And I am five years old once more.

Sliabh Meadhonach – The Great Loneliness

In the far west of the island there is a part that has no name in English. It is a part rather than a single place. I like to enter it just north of Port Ban, and entering feels the right way to describe it. It feels an ancient landscape, unchanged from the beginning of time. It's made of high rocky outcrops and tiny winding glens. There's a beauty about it despite its ruggedness; the deep green of the little glens contrasts with the dark browns and blacks of the rocks. And in June and July these little glens are filled with a profusion of wild flowers: orchids and bog cotton and myrtle. In the marshy pools there are flag irises. Meadow pipits, linnets and wheatears flutter from rock to rock, and often the coal voice of a raven will echo as one of the great black birds ripples across the sky. Somehow it feels like a Biblical landscape, the kind of place where the prophets hid away in their caves and listened. Little doubt that the Celts, too, must have seen it as a kind of desert, a place where heaven and earth came close. For almost at the very heart of this great loneliness is the Hermit's Cell.

The Hermit's Cell

The Abbey

How many centuries did this place
Let in the storm and rain? A refuge for cattle
In the raging of a four day gale.
Did a mother hurry here
Under cover of dark with a failing child,
To stand in the sanctuary broken,
And pray he might be well again?
Or was the place all passed as Popish ruin
Best left broken, the old remains of Irishness?
Now it's back where it belongs –
The whispers left inside the stone intact.

During the war years, the work on the rebuilding of Iona Abbey continued. But now all timber was required for the war effort; where was wood going to be found for the work? It would be hard not to see what took place as anything short of a miracle. A ship crossing the sea from Canada ran into a storm. The deck cargo, which was timber, was jettisoned for safety. It floated eighty miles and was washed ashore on Mull – opposite Iona. The wood was even the perfect length.

Ron Ferguson tells in his book on the story of the Iona Community, *Chasing the Wild Goose*, of an amazing sight. Not a Viking longship storming towards Iona, but rather a ship that was bringing timber – fine, Scandinavian wood – for the refectory of the Abbey. It was a present from Norway – from the Church and from industry – a thousand years after the Viking raids.

When I was four or five
I believed the cloister on Iona
Was the centre of the world.

No-one had told me, I just knew
And looked through the carved pillars
Into the light of the sky inside.

And once upon a time
I suppose, in a strange way –
It was.

Wells

They were seen as holy by the early Celts, long before the
Christian Gospel came to Ireland. They were sacred long
before that, for what could be more magical than pure, clear
water bubbling from the darkness of the earth? And that
water would be more than likely full, too, of precious
minerals bringing wholeness and healing. The water of
particular springs and wells became known for its healing of
certain conditions: toothache, whooping cough and a
hundred other ailments. Even madness might be cured by it.

With the arrival of Christianity came a faith that had plenty
to say about wells and healing. The old processions to
springs on certain days were not forbidden; rather they were
incorporated into the new order of things. Springs and wells
were christened; they were called after saints and their
healing power ascribed to them.

The Well of the North Wind, the Well of Eternal Youth, the
Well at the Dell of the Cock and the Hill of the Well – all
these beautifully evocative names are from Iona. But of all
of them, it's surely the first that sounds most powerful and
beautiful of all. Evidently, sailors used to visit the well (to be
found not far from the Hermit's Cell), when they were
becalmed. There they made offerings and prayed that a
north wind might rise and take them on their way.

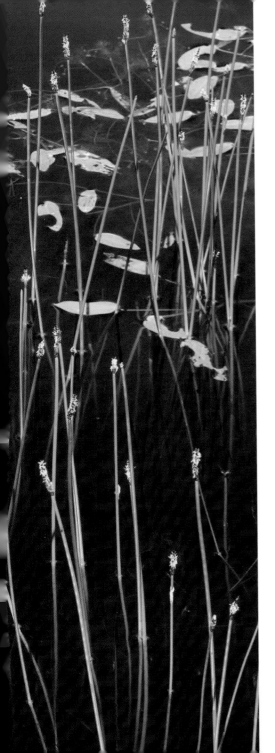

The Well of the North Wind

Still night and the dark down
the islands lying at anchor asleep.
The orchids nodding their heads
in the summer's breath about me.
And I am here with a brooch of gold,
I am kneeling in the soft earth
To ask for a north wind
for a ship with sails that will not stir.
For men who are hungry for home,
who would walk the water now if they could;
Whose hands are sore
for the holding of love, who yearn
All they have not known
these long months gone.
And so I come seeking a north wind
this morning, as the shadows lift
And a dragon's eye of dawn
grows bright and gold in the east.

Dun Ì

Recently, I heard visitors to Iona (from mainland Scotland) describing the highest point on the island as a mountain. I confess to having been rather amused; Dun Ì (the Ì is pronounced 'ee') is far more a molehill than a mountain.

On a good, clear day it's still worth slogging up its steep slopes to the summit. Of course the views to all manner of islands are breath-taking; in fact standing on that summit makes you aware just what a heart-stone Iona is, nestled between the sea roads at the very centre of that fragmented Hebridean world.

But look also to your feet, for there close to the cairn is the Well of Eternal Youth. Look carefully, for it's easy to overlook as a rather unprepossessing puddle. I would love to know the origin of the name, whether it really does date back to the high days of the Celts, or whether it's one of the more fanciful later names coined once the misty romanticism of Ossian had swirled about Highland Scotland.

The story is, of course, that Columba chose Iona because, from here, he couldn't see Ireland. I smile rather at that and think that it must have been a dreich day when he landed, because from the summit of Dun Ì on a truly clear day it's certainly possible to see Malin Head.

The Dutchman's Cap

Mull from the
top of Dun

The North End

Iona's North End feels like many little places rather than one single one. There are tiny fragments of coves, little rocky promontories and great sweeps of white sand. There are many for whom the North End is simply their first reconnection with Iona after long absence: that pilgrimage must be made before anything else is done.

Whenever I walk north I think of the Colourist painters who chose Iona for that wondrous quality of light and came to capture it. Sometimes they went so far as to tie themselves to rocks to get as close to a capturing of the wild sea as possible. And it's the views north, to the magnificent cliffs of Burg on Mull and all the wonderful weird-shaped clutter of volcanic debris, that comes to mind when I think of those artists.

There's all too little to remember them today on Iona. I would like to know the cottages where they lived and more about the whole story of their stay. It's certain that in those days of Presbyterian strictness, their avant-garde living must have shocked the good folk of Iona. Painting would have seemed a sinful waste of time when harvests of oats and fish had to be gathered in days that were a sheer fight for survival.

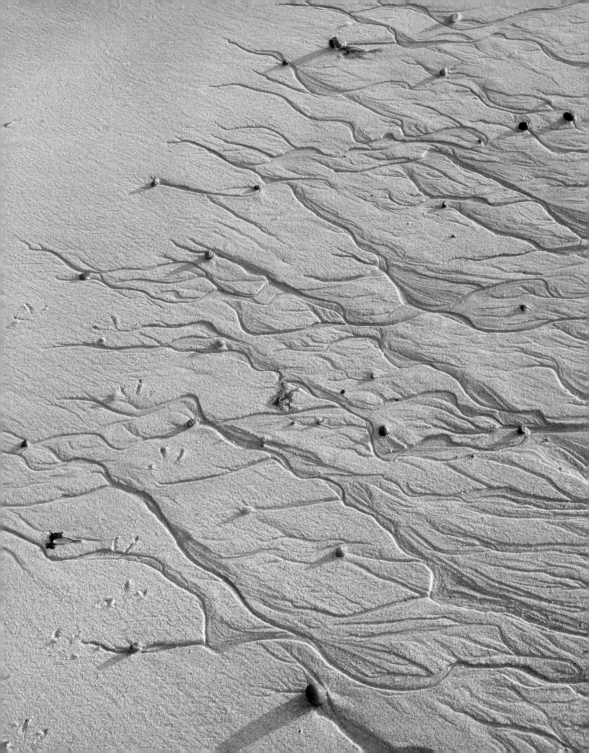

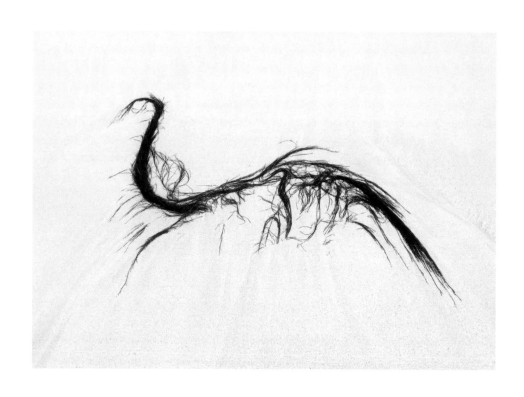

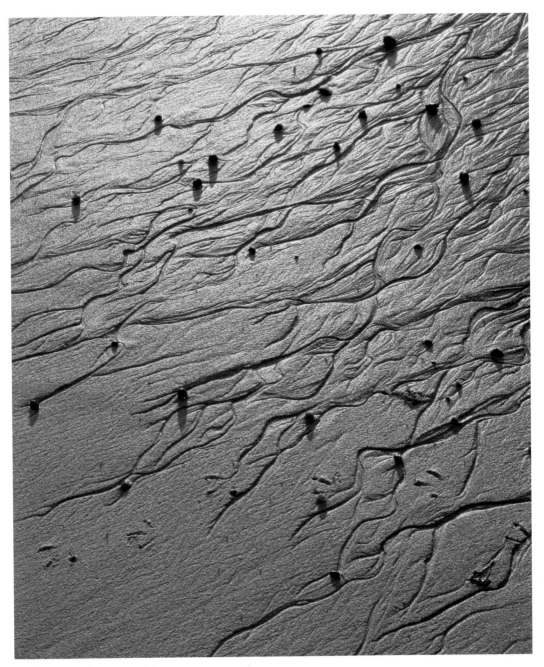

We asked four people who either live, or have lived, on Iona, to describe their chosen corner of the island and explain why it is so special to them. The following are their own accounts.

The South West Corner – *Helen Steven*

My first introduction to the South West Corner of Iona came as something of a surprise. I had just started work for the Iona Community as their Justice and Peace Worker when I met Roger Gray. Roger was an optician in Portree in the Isle of Skye. He was also a dedicated and passionate peace campaigner, so when he grabbed my arm and said he wanted to share a very special secret with me, I didn't know what to expect, but trustingly I plunged over bogs and rocks with him. His secret was the nesting fulmars at the South West Corner, and as I lay beside him peering over the cliffs at the wheeling, soaring fulmars I knew it was indeed a very special place.

The South West Corner is possibly the most remote part of the island. To get there, head up to Loch Staonaig, then up to the Cairn of the Back to Ireland. Going SW from there one reaches a seemingly impassable rampart of cliffs with a peninsula of wild land spread out alluringly below. It is possible to climb down the cliffs in one or two places, but it is not really recommended. Instead follow the cliffs to their southern end where it is easier to turn then.

And then you are there, with a feeling of having stepped into another world with a special magic that is all your own. The heather here is deeper and rougher because of less grazing and I once found a startlingly bright clump of white heather – surely a sign of acceptance. The coastline here is particularly rugged and even on the calmest of days there is a constant surge of foaming white against the ancient red rocks. Indeed when we sing the line of the hymn *St Patrick's Breastplate*, it is always these rocks that my inner eye is seeing. Struggle to the

The whirling wind's tempestuous shocks,
The stable earth, the deep salt sea
Around the old eternal rocks

South West Corner in a good-going westerly gale and the crashing of the waves and the tearing of the wind is spectacular.

But for me the escape from the somewhat frenetic life at the Abbey is best enjoyed on a calm day. Then one can sit for ages absolutely alone watching the fulmars as they wheel silently closer, eyeing the intruder with a baleful eye. Perhaps it was this peace and solitude that the Celtic monks were seeking when they journeyed to remote islands and skerries. Who knows, even Columba himself might have sought prayerful solitude here in the South West Corner.

The Second Ark – *Alastair McIntosh*

It was in the late 1980s that I first stumbled upon the Great Forest of Iona. I'd wandered down to the south-east corner that the map shows as *Sliabh Siar* – the Mountains of the West.

You'll say there is no great forest on Iona, there are no mountains, and that the south-east is not the west! But look again. Look from the mainland, and all of Iona lies west. Look in Dwelly's dictionary, and the Gaelic, *sliabh*, meaning 'mountain of the first magnitude,' morphs to moorland heath and even down to the 'moor bent grass'.

As for the oaks, it was just two or three trees that I found on the lips of treacherous holes and gullies near the Marble Quarry. Wizened and stunted to chest-height, their tops lay bent almost as right angles from the winter gales.

According to a medieval Irish tract, the *Betha Colaim Cille*, whenever an oak tree blew down St Columba would tell his followers not to chop it up 'till the end of nine days, and then to divide it among all the folk of the place, good and bad; a third part of it to be put in the guest-house for the guests, and a tenth part as a share for the poor'.

It was from oak that he built his church on Iona. He built another in Ireland by an oak copse, and so confined was the plot that he orientated the building north-south instead of east-west 'so loath was he to cut down the grove'.

A seventh-century contemporary of our Celtic monks was Isaac of Syria. As today's civil war raged in that country my thoughts turned to his words: 'The ark of Noah was built in the time of peace, and its timbers were planted by him a hundred years beforehand'.

It made me think of Columba's dying words as reported by St Adomnan: 'Love one another unfeignedly. Peace.' And how, Adomnan said, he destined to 'lead the nations until life'.

These seeds of peace are acorns set in holy ground. Their oaks, though bent and battered by the gales, are hanging on in hidden boles and gullies of both east and west.

One day we'll find the eyes to see them as great forests. And that day, which is perhaps this day, shall be a great day: for God shall set our hands to build the Second Ark.

On wanting to go to the Hermit's Cell –
Ali Campbell

I *want* to go to the Hermit's Cell. People say it moves: indeed two people I know say they have never found it. But I always find it, although I never seem to go by the same path twice.

It's my special place, that quiet circle. I heal there. Once a year, on my annual pilgrimage to Iona, on a day that changes every year but – finally – always comes, I start off across the little moor beyond the MacLeod Centre, larks scintillating in an otherwise silent sky, the sun flashing up from black pools lined with peat ...

... and arrive. But not today. A beaming couple hove into view, vividly weatherproofed trousers swishing cheerfully as they go. Headed for my special place! I'm discombobulated. I *want* it to myself. One day out of 365: is that too much to ask?

As I swither there, quite thrown ('swither': somewhere between switching and dithering), a sudden high keening spins me round and up and out of myself. My eyes follow and there's a buzzard! – swerving and tracking along the shoulders of Dun Ì.

Another cry! – another bird: the mate. They're alternating as a team, one roosting on a high point of rock I've never seen before, the other systematically mapping the wind, quartering the moor, watching the world below. Small furry creatures beware! There must be a hungry nest nearby. For a second I am passed over, glanced at, forgotten. Inedible maybe?

Where was I going again? I seem to have found a new path. That, or it's found me. The buzzard's shadow draws my eye along this path and up, between shining grasses, looping along the hillside. The path curves back towards the farm below Dun Ì.

I've never been this way before. I pass a revelation of orchids as the dull sky brightens. Marsh cotton tufts dance white, whiter, whitest, just above the earth.

Another cry! – the buzzard swoops again, the roosting one heraldic: an emblem of watchfulness above me. The path widens ... to a track lined with old railway sleepers, funnelling downwards to a field where they dip sheep.

Another turn, and one last cry. I'm standing on a high saddle of green, by a low pile of timber, silvered with age, warm from the veiled but still-bright sun. Flickering reeds in a ring whisper around this plain, tidy stack: a circle squared.

I'm sitting, then lying, then asleep before I know it, in a place I didn't *want* to go to, circles of air and light and sound around me and above, old warm wood at my back, at the end of the path that found me. Not where I wanted to go. But where I need to be.

The Dappled Dell (*An Uiridh Riabhach*) –
Joyce Watson

One of my favourite places on Iona (and it's hard to single out any one) is 'the Dappled Dell'. What a lovely name, conjuring up visions of a bluebell wood in springtime, sunlight filtering gently through fresh green beech leaves.

Not so! I wonder how this bleak, wild and remote part of Iona got its name?

Many years ago a friend took me there. We walked across wild moorland to the South West Corner of Iona, made a careful descent via a narrow path down the cliff-side, after which there was a certain amount of scrambling over slippery rocks. We arrived at a deep, sheer-sided inlet, at the foot of high rock cliffs. Waves seethed in and out, and from the foot of the cliff there came a sloshing and gurgling sound: 'Like a pig having a bath,' said Mahala.

In more recent years, another friend and I were enjoying a picnic on a hilltop above St Columba's Bay on a blustery winter's day when suddenly, away towards the west, a great plume of water shot skywards. Just like the well-known Spouting Cave by the Machair. It had to be a second spouting cave. How exciting! The light was fading so we needed to start back, but the next day, early in the morning, we went to find it. I soon realised that we were heading towards the Dappled Dell, and I could hear the same sloshing and gurgling, but there was no water spout.

However, we could see a fissure in the cliff, and a hollow space below, and reckoned that, given the right state of tide and sufficient swell, water would be forced dramatically up and out as the waves surged in. To catch it spouting became our project, and each year when Morven returned for her annual visit we would set off, with sandwiches, flasks of hot drinks, and cameras. All to no avail it seemed, until at last we made it at just the right time and sat in awe watching the dramatic spectacle.

Now we need to find a new project!

Why is it a favourite place? Certainly it evokes happy memories of adventures with dear friends. And perhaps because it is a place of raw, untamed, savage beauty; a dramatic contrast to places I also love, like the peaceful, beautiful Port Ban.

Sometimes I need wild places!

Port of the Ox Rock

Port of Ivor's Cornfield

122

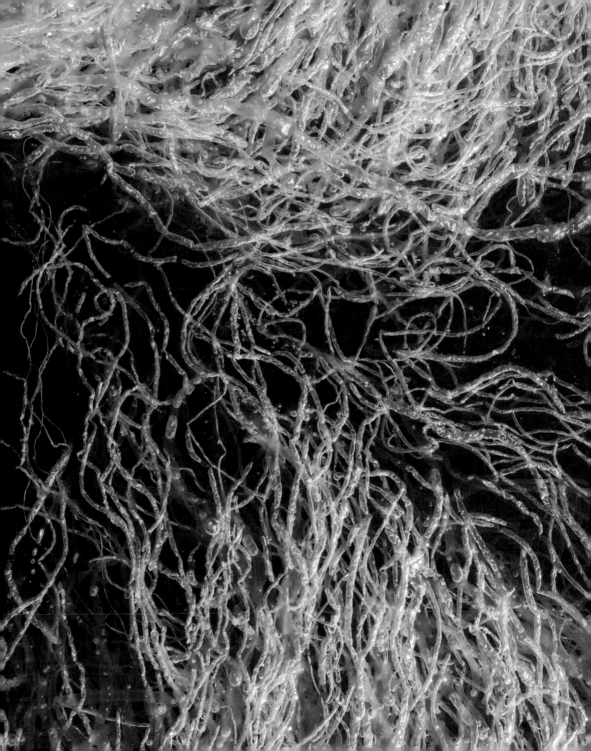